CORE LIBRARY OF US STATES

SOUTH DAKOTA

BY HELEN EVANS WALSH

CONTENT CONSULTANT
Michael J. Mullin, PhD
Professor of History
Augustana University

Core Library

An Imprint of Abdo Publishing
abdobooks.com

abdobooks.com

Published by Abdo Publishing, a division of ABDO, PO Box 398166, Minneapolis, Minnesota 55439.

Printed in the United States of America, North Mankato, Minnesota.
052022
092022

THIS BOOK CONTAINS RECYCLED MATERIALS

Cover Photo: Shutterstock Images
Interior Photos: Shutterstock Images, 4–5, 15, 21 (flag), 21 (flower), 22–23, 27, 43, 45; Red Line Editorial, 7 (South Dakota), 7 (USA); Jacob Boomsma/Shutterstock Images, 9, 39, 40; Sarin Images/Granger Historical Picture Archive, 12–13; Photo Researchers/Science History Images/Alamy, 19; Steve Byland/Shutterstock Images, 21 (coyote); Marcin Perkowski/Shutterstock Images, 21 (bird); Vladimir Shulikovskiy/Shutterstock Images, 21 (tree); Carol Mellema/Shutterstock Images, 28–29; Patrick Ziegler/Shutterstock Images, 32; AP Images, 34–35

Editor: Arnold Ringstad
Series Designer: Joshua Olson

Library of Congress Control Number: 2021951566

Publisher's Cataloging-in-Publication Data

Names: Evans Walsh, Helen, author.
Title: South Dakota / by Helen Evans Walsh
Description: Minneapolis, Minnesota : Abdo Publishing, 2023 | Series: Core library of US states | Includes online resources and index.
Identifiers: ISBN 9781532197833 (lib. bdg.) | ISBN 9781098270599 (ebook)
Subjects: LCSH: U.S. states--Juvenile literature. | Midwest States--Juvenile literature. | South Dakota--History--Juvenile literature. | Physical geography--United States--Juvenile literature.
Classification: DDC 978.3--dc23

Population demographics broken down by race and ethnicity come from the 2019 census estimate. Population totals come from the 2020 census.

CONTENTS

CHAPTER ONE

THE MOUNT RUSHMORE STATE

As the sun rises, orange, yellow, and red rays of light bathe the four stone faces carved into Mount Rushmore. The mountain sculpture features four of America's greatest presidents: George Washington, Thomas Jefferson, Theodore Roosevelt, and Abraham Lincoln. Each president's head stretches 60 feet (18 m) tall. The presidents represent the history, determination, and achievements of the country and its people.

More than 450,000 tons (408,000 metric tons) of rock were removed during the sculpting of Mount Rushmore.

CREATING MOUNT RUSHMORE

Creating Mount Rushmore was a massive project. A sculptor named Gutzon Borglum designed the monument. He chose the Black Hills region of South Dakota for its dramatic setting. Carving of the mountain began in 1927. Workers used dynamite to remove rock and roughly carve the presidential faces. For more detailed parts, they used air hammers. They completed Washington in 1930, Jefferson in 1936, Lincoln in 1937, and Roosevelt in 1939. The entire project was finished in 1941.

Every year more than 2 million people visit Mount Rushmore. Visitors can view the mountain sculpture from an amphitheater. They can also take a short walk along the Presidential Trail or hike to the Borglum View Terrace for different views of the monument. Some people visit the nearby Sculptor's Studio. There they can listen to park rangers talk about the life of sculptor Gutzon Borglum and the carving process that created the presidential sculpture. This famous monument is why South Dakota is known as the Mount Rushmore State.

MAP OF SOUTH DAKOTA

South Dakota has important historic sites and beautiful landscapes. How does this map help you understand all that the state has to offer?

ABOUT SOUTH DAKOTA

South Dakota is part of the Midwest region of the United States. It shares borders with several states. Minnesota and Iowa are to the east. A long border in the south separates South Dakota from Nebraska. In the west the state touches Wyoming and Montana. And to the north is North Dakota.

South Dakota is the sixteenth-largest state in the United States, covering 77,116 square miles (199,730 sq km). Some people call it the Land of Infinite Variety. That is because South Dakota has a great diversity in its weather, geography, economy, and more.

SOUTH DAKOTA'S REGIONS

South Dakota can be divided into the west, central, northeast, and southeast regions. The west is home to the Badlands and the Black Hills. People explore caves, forests, and mountain peaks. Mount Rushmore is also found in the west region. Rapid City is a gateway to these attractions.

Pierre is one of the nation's smallest state capitals, with around 14,000 people.

South Dakota's capital city, Pierre (pronounced PEER), is located in the central region. The Missouri River runs through the central region. In the 1940s the river was dammed to create several large reservoirs. These include the Oahe, Francis Case, Sharpe, and Lewis and Clark reservoirs. Many people travel to the river and reservoirs for water recreation.

The northeast region is home to glacial lakes and prairies. It offers many outdoor activities. Aberdeen, the state's third-largest city, is in this region. Watertown is another busy city in the Northeast. There is a museum there for artist Terry Redlin. It displays more than 150 pieces of his art.

South Dakota's biggest city, Sioux Falls, is in the southeast region. Waterfalls on the Big Sioux River rush through the city.

Outside of South Dakota's cities, farms and small towns make up most of the land. In the southeast there are 175 fishing lakes. People can walk through vineyards or explore a historic route on the Missouri River. Natural beauty and human-made sites alike attract many people to South Dakota.

PERSPECTIVES

TERRY REDLIN

Artist Terry Redlin was born in South Dakota in 1937. He loved the outdoors. At age 15, he lost a leg in a motorcycle accident. He became passionate about art and later became a popular wildlife artist. His son Charles had the idea for a gallery dedicated to his father's work. The Redlin Art Center opened in Watertown in 1997. Charles said, "Since South Dakota sent Dad through art school on a scholarship for disabled students, he wanted to build it in Watertown as a gift to the state and the community." Terry Redlin died in 2016 at age 78.

STRAIGHT TO THE SOURCE

Journalist John Taliaferro wrote a book about the history of Mount Rushmore. In 2020 he spoke to a public radio station about the monument, including what it means to American Indians:

> *To Native Americans, Mount Rushmore is not a poke in the eye—it's a poke in the heart. This land that Mount Rushmore is on was given to the Sioux by the US Congress in 1868, permanent ownership, then taken away from them. . . . Rushmore, like the Statue of Liberty, is meant to be sort of shorthand for what America is. But it's not, it's more complicated than that.*

Source: Peter O'Dowd and Serena McMahon. "Mount Rushmore Historian: Monument 'Is Like a Rorschach, It Says Different Things to Different People.'" *WBUR*, 1 July 2020, wbur.org. Accessed 9 Aug. 2021.

WHAT'S THE BIG IDEA?

Read the above passage carefully. What is the main point Taliaferro is trying to make? Why does he describe Mount Rushmore as complicated?

CHAPTER TWO

HISTORY OF SOUTH DAKOTA

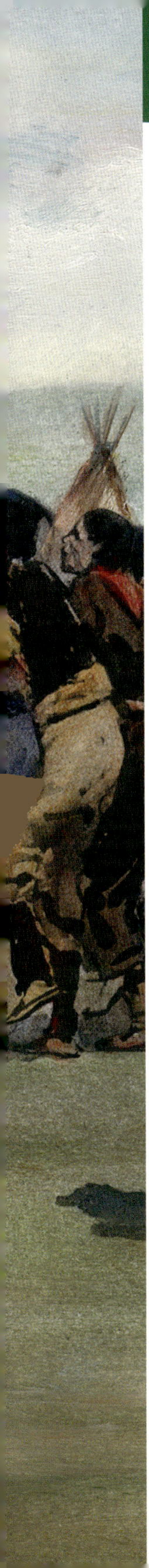

People have lived in South Dakota for about 10,000 years. Researchers believe early peoples hunted large animals, such as bison, to survive. The Mandan and Arikara peoples later settled on these lands. By 1770 the Oceti Sakowin (Sioux) dominated the area. Different communities spoke the Dakota, Lakota, or Nakota languages. They lived in tepees and gathered plants. They also hunted bison, trapped beaver, and fished.

An 1890 painting by artist Frederic Remington depicts an Oglala Sioux religious dance known as the Ghost Dance.

EUROPEAN COLONISTS ARRIVE

In the 1700s French explorers arrived in what is now South Dakota. They claimed this land for France in 1743. For many years the British, French, and Spanish argued over it. Then in 1803 the French sold a large area of land to the United States. It included the area that would become South Dakota. This deal was known as the Louisiana Purchase.

Fort Pierre is one of the state's oldest permanent European settlements. It was built in 1832. Later in the 1800s, white Americans started to settle in South Dakota. They built homes and farms.

FUTHER LAND DISPUTES

In the 1800s the Oceti Sakowin struggled against the US government. The government wanted to limit where the Oceti Sakowin could live. The government made treaties with the Oceti Sakowin. But these deals favored the government. These treaties ended the Oceti Sakowin people's freedom to live wherever they chose.

Many American Indian peoples have historic connections to the Black Hills region of South Dakota.

In 1861 the United States named an area north and east of the Missouri River the Dakota Territory. It was a large region. It included land that would later become North Dakota, South Dakota, and parts of three other states. The territory's original capital was Yankton, located on the Missouri River.

In that same year, some Southern states broke away to form the Confederacy. They wanted to keep the practice of slavery. The Northern states, called the Union, went to war to reunite the country. The two sides fought in the American Civil War (1861–1865). After the Union victory, more treaties and agreements gave tribal lands to the US government. In the Treaty of 1868, the US government created the Great Sioux Reservation, which included the Black Hills.

As more settlers arrived, conflicts between the Lakota nation and the settlers occurred. Then in 1874 a military expedition discovered gold in the Black Hills. Soon after, gold fever struck the area. People traveled there from all around to find the precious metal. The US government forced the Lakota to give up the Black Hills.

In 1877 the Black Hills were made a part of the Dakota Territory. The Great Sioux Reservation became smaller. The Lakota argued that the Black Hills belonged to them. But the government wanted gold. It did not stop miners from flooding the area. American Indian religious practices caused more tensions in relations with the US government.

In 1890 the US military clashed with the Oceti Sakowin near the town of Wounded Knee. More than 250 Oceti Sakowin men, women, and children were killed. The event became known as the Wounded Knee Massacre. After the massacre, the Oceti Sakowin found themselves isolated on their reservations.

PERSPECTIVES

SACRED SITE

For the Lakota people, the Black Hills are a sacred site. Lakota scholar Vine Deloria says, "In the spring, the people would follow the buffalo herd and they'd have to do a series of four ceremonies, the last one of which would either end up at Devils Tower or Bear Butte depending on what year it was and what the situation was." The Lakota continue to hold ceremonies at Bear Butte, or Mato Paha. To the Lakota, the Black Hills are Paha Sapa, meaning "the heart of everything that is."

STATEHOOD

On November 2, 1889, the growing Dakota Territory was granted statehood. The territory was divided into two states: North Dakota and South Dakota. President Benjamin Harrison signed the documents that made them states. He shuffled the paperwork, so no one knows which one became a state first. South Dakota is either the thirty-ninth or fortieth state. In 1904 Pierre became South Dakota's state capital.

In the state's early days, agriculture was a major part of life. People grew crops and raised cattle. In the 1920s and 1930s, drought and dust storms dried up farmland. Powerful winds blew topsoil from the land. This time was known as the Dust Bowl. Farmers were unable to grow and harvest crops. Many people and businesses were devastated.

During the mid-1900s, flooding of the Missouri River caused damage. The government responded by building more than 50 dams on the Missouri River.

Dust storms buried machinery in Dallas, South Dakota, during the Dust Bowl.

These were meant to control floods. The dams also brought water and electricity to farms.

In the 1970s a civil rights movement for better treatment of American Indian people swept the United States. American Indians, including Oceti Sakowin nations, brought back religious traditions. These activists also challenged the leadership of local reservations. In 1973 a group of American Indian activists occupied the town of Wounded Knee. They wanted to drive the chairman of the Pine Ridge Reservation from power. Police surrounded the town. Two activists died, and people on both sides were injured by gunfire. After 71 days, the occupation ended. The activists surrendered.

TRIBES AND GOVERNMENT

South Dakota is home to nine federally recognized American Indian tribes. The Cheyenne River Sioux Tribe has the largest reservation by area. The Oglala Sioux and Rosebud Sioux Tribes are the state's largest in population. They have tens of thousands of members each.

SD'S FIRST FEMALE GOVERNOR

In 2018 Kristi Noem was elected the first female governor of South Dakota. She grew up in South Dakota. Starting in 2007, Noem served in the state's House of Representatives for four years. Then in 2011, she became South Dakota's only representative in the US House of Representatives. She was the second woman ever elected to this position.

South Dakota's state government has three branches. The legislative branch writes laws. It is made up of a Senate and a House of Representatives. The executive branch is led by the governor and other state officials. The judicial branch is the court system.

SOUTH DAKOTA
QUICK FACTS

Take a look at the state symbols of South Dakota. How do they help you understand the state's geography and wildlife?

Abbreviation: SD
Nickname: The Mount Rushmore State
Motto: Under God the people rule
Date of statehood: November 2, 1889
Capital: Pierre
Population: 886,667
Area: 77,116 square miles (199,730 sq km)

STATE SYMBOLS

State animal
Coyote

State flower
American pasque

State bird
Ring-necked pheasant

State tree
Black Hills spruce

CHAPTER THREE

GEOGRAPHY AND CLIMATE

South Dakota has variety in its geography and climate. The Missouri River splits the state roughly in half. In the east, large plains stretch across flat land. Floodplains along the river have fertile soil, making these areas ideal for farming. In the northeast, lakes are scattered across the land. Glaciers formed them thousands of years ago.

The Black Hills are an exception to South Dakota's flat land. Those southwest peaks include Black Elk Peak. This is the highest

Rocks in Badlands National Park are approximately 75 million years old.

PERSPECTIVES

CLIMATE CHANGE IN SOUTH DAKOTA

Climate change is the gradual warming of Earth's average temperature. It is caused by greenhouse gases that trap heat in the atmosphere. In South Dakota, climate change is causing more rain. More rain may help crops and plants grow. But too much rain can run off and not soak into the soil. Warmer temperatures mean the snow melts faster. Less water flows later in the summer for irrigation. Warm weather also dries out the ground, causing problems for farmers and plants. Hotter summers could also be dangerous for people and animals. Cows eat less when they are hot, so they grow slower and make less beef for food.

point in North America east of the Rocky Mountains. It rises 7,244 feet (2,208 m) high. Forests cover many of the hillsides. Black Hills National Forest is found here.

Also in the southwest part of the state, the Badlands rise above the flat prairie land. The Badlands are jagged, rocky hills called gullies. The name Badlands comes from white explorers. They called the region "bad land" because it was difficult to cross and hard to farm.

South Dakota experiences four distinct seasons. Summers are hot and sometimes humid. Fall has crisp, cool nights. Winters are cold and snowy. In the spring, the weather is mild. The climate depends on location. The east generally experiences more precipitation and humidity, while the western part of the state is drier.

PLANTS AND ANIMALS

Many kinds of plants and animals live in South Dakota's habitats. Larger animals are found on the western side of the state. These include elk, deer, beavers, and bobcats. Many depend on forests for food and shelter. Deer eat only plants. Bobcats are carnivores that hunt for smaller animals. Bison, coyotes, and cottontail rabbits live on the plains.

Several types of fish and birds live throughout the state. Trout, pike, perch, and bass swim in lakes and streams. Bald eagles, golden eagles, and pheasants

BISON

Bison are sometimes called buffalo, but that is not their official name. Bison are the heaviest land animals in the United States. They can weigh more than 1 ton (0.91 metric tons). Yet their size does not slow them down. Bison can run up to 40 miles per hour (64 km/h).

Millions of bison once lived in the Midwest. White settlers killed about 50 million bison in the 1800s. Only a small number of the animals remained. Since then, people have worked to protect the bison. Now their numbers have rebounded to about 500,000 that live on preserves and ranches.

soar above. Ducks and geese fly along the Missouri River during their migrations.

The Black Hills spruce is also known as the white spruce. It is found in the region that shares its name. Thick, tall grasses cover prairies across the state. They grow 3 feet (1 m) tall. Deep roots help the grasses store water. The American pasque grows on the prairies too. Its bright purple flower was historically used for healing by American Indians and early settlers. Shorter grasses grow on plains. Plains

Sharp-tailed grouse are native to South Dakota. This type of bird is known for its mating dance.

tend to be flatter and drier than prairies. Short grasses are less likely to dry out. They have shallow roots so they can quickly sprout up.

EXPLORE ONLINE

Chapter Three discusses the climate of South Dakota. The website below goes into more depth on this topic and how climate change will impact the state. Does the website answer any questions you had about South Dakota's climate and how climate change may affect it?

WHAT CLIMATE CHANGE MEANS FOR SOUTH DAKOTA

abdocorelibrary.com/south-dakota

CHAPTER FOUR

RESOURCES AND ECONOMY

South Dakota is rich in natural resources. Mining in the state produces construction materials such as limestone, granite, sand, clay, crushed stone, and gravel. The state is also a source of gypsum and natural gas. Until the early 2000s, South Dakota was a leading producer of gold in the United States. Today gold mining still takes place, but on a smaller scale.

South Dakota produces millions of pounds of sunflower products each year.

BLACK HILLS GOLD

In 1988 South Dakota named Black Hills gold as the official state jewelry. Black Hills gold is made only in South Dakota. Each piece of jewelry features a pattern of gold swirls, grapes, and leaves. The leaves are made of combinations of green, rose, and yellow gold. To create the distinctive colors of Black Hills gold jewelry, jewelry makers mix 24-carat gold with other metals. To create the green color, gold and sterling silver are mixed. To make a rose color, jewelers blend copper and gold.

AGRICULTURE, INDUSTRY, AND TOURISM

In addition to mining, agriculture is an important part of South Dakota's economy. It is the state's largest industry. There are more than 31,000 farms and ranches across the state. South Dakota ranks in the top ten states for producing hay, sunflowers, rye, wheat, honey, corn, soybeans, and cattle. Farms in the north are known for growing crops, especially corn and wheat. Southern farms raise cattle and livestock. The Black Hills also produce lumber.

Most of South Dakota's farms and ranches are family owned and operated. The average farm is about 1,395 acres (565 ha). The average South Dakota farmer produces enough food to feed 155 people for a year.

Energy and manufacturing are other parts of the economy. River dams help create hydroelectric power. Factories make wood and electronic products. South Dakota also has several meat and dairy processing plants. Baking and

PERSPECTIVES

A FARMING FAMILY

For Larry Aker, farming is a family venture. His family has farmed in South Dakota for more than 100 years. Aker's grandparents started the farm in 1920. Larry himself has been farming for more than 50 years. Today his son works with him. The Akers primarily grow corn and soybeans. They also raise cattle. The weather is always a worry. Aker remembers the drought of 1976 as one of the worst. "I remember the crops were started, and then it froze—froze a lot of them off. And then [we] never got any rain after that. There just wasn't much of anything," Aker said. "No crops and very little hay."

Gavins Point Dam is a hydroelectric dam that lies between South Dakota and Nebraska.

flour-milling companies are located throughout the state. Many people are employed in manufacturing, health care, and retail.

Tourism is a key part of South Dakota's economy. In 2019 more than 14 million tourists visited South Dakota.

Visitors bring in lots of money for the state and also create many jobs. People travel to South Dakota to visit natural and historic sites. Mount Rushmore and the Crazy Horse Memorial are the top tourist spots. One major event is the annual motorcycle rally in Sturgis. Hundreds of thousands of bikers come to the event each year.

FURTHER EVIDENCE

Chapter Four discusses agriculture and South Dakota's economy. Identify one of the author's main points. What evidence does the author provide to support this point? The website at the link below also discusses the topic. Find a quote on this website that supports the author's main point. Does it offer a new piece of evidence?

SOUTH DAKOTA AGRICULTURE

abdocorelibrary.com/south-dakota

CHAPTER FIVE

PEOPLE AND PLACES

In 2020 nearly 900,000 people lived in South Dakota. White people who are not Hispanic or Latino make up about 80 percent of the population. The next largest racial and ethnic groups are American Indian or Alaska Native at 9 percent and Hispanic or Latino at 4 percent. About 2 percent of South Dakotans are Black, and about 1.5 percent are Asian.

About half of South Dakota's population lives in cities. The other half lives in rural areas,

Russell Means, a member of the Oglala Sioux Tribe, spoke out about US government treaties with American Indian nations.

on reservations, or in religious communities. Tens of thousands of American Indians live on nine reservations in the state.

PERSPECTIVES

FOOD AND CULTURE

South Dakota's state dessert is a German-Russian pastry called kuchen. It was brought by the immigrants who moved to the state in the 1880s. Kuchen is a dough pie made with custard. Sometimes it features fruits such as peaches, raisins, or apples. Other times kuchen is savory and made with cottage cheese, sauerkraut, or onions. Kuchen is usually topped with streusel, cinnamon, sugar, or almonds. It was common for Germans to get together for coffee and kuchen during the day. The tradition continued in South Dakota.

Famous people from South Dakota include former news anchor Tom Brokaw, actress January Jones, author Laura Ingalls Wilder, and professional football player Adam Vinatieri. American Indian activist Russell Means was born in the state. Pro wrestler Shayna Baszler and Olympic runner Billy Mills are from South Dakota too.

PLACES TO VISIT

There is a lot to see and do in South Dakota. The state is rich in history. Many people visit Mount Rushmore to see the enormous faces of the presidents. At the Crazy Horse Memorial in Crazy Horse, South Dakota, visitors can see a mountain carving in progress. Once complete, this carving of the Lakota leader will be the largest mountain carving in the world. Visitors can also follow the trail of explorers Lewis and Clark and trace their steps across South Dakota. The town of Deadwood has an Old West theme with historic

CRAZY HORSE MEMORIAL

The Crazy Horse Memorial is located in the Black Hills. Sculptor Korczak Ziolkowski began the mountain carving project in 1948. Crazy Horse was a chief of the Oglala Lakota. He was a warrior during the mid-1800s. The memorial has proven controversial. Some Lakota people, including some of Crazy Horse's descendants, oppose it. They say that no one asked the family for approval before the project began.

storefronts and live reenactments on Main Street. In Pierre people can visit the Museum of the South Dakota State Historical Society.

The state's natural attractions also draw many people to South Dakota. The Black Hills are home to a variety of outdoor activities. Beneath the Black Hills, Jewel Cave is one of the largest cave systems in the world. Archaeology fans can visit Mammoth Site, a museum in Hot Springs. It shows off 61 mammoth skeletons uncovered by scientists. Those with an interest in mining can visit Homestake Mine. It is one of the largest, deepest gold mines in the world. The mine is also home to the Sanford Underground Research Facility. Here scientists perform sensitive experiments deep below the surface of the Earth.

Badlands National Park features dramatic landscapes. Herds of bison roam through the park. On scenic drives and hikes, visitors can explore the park's

Visitors can see educational displays alongside the fossils at Mammoth Site.

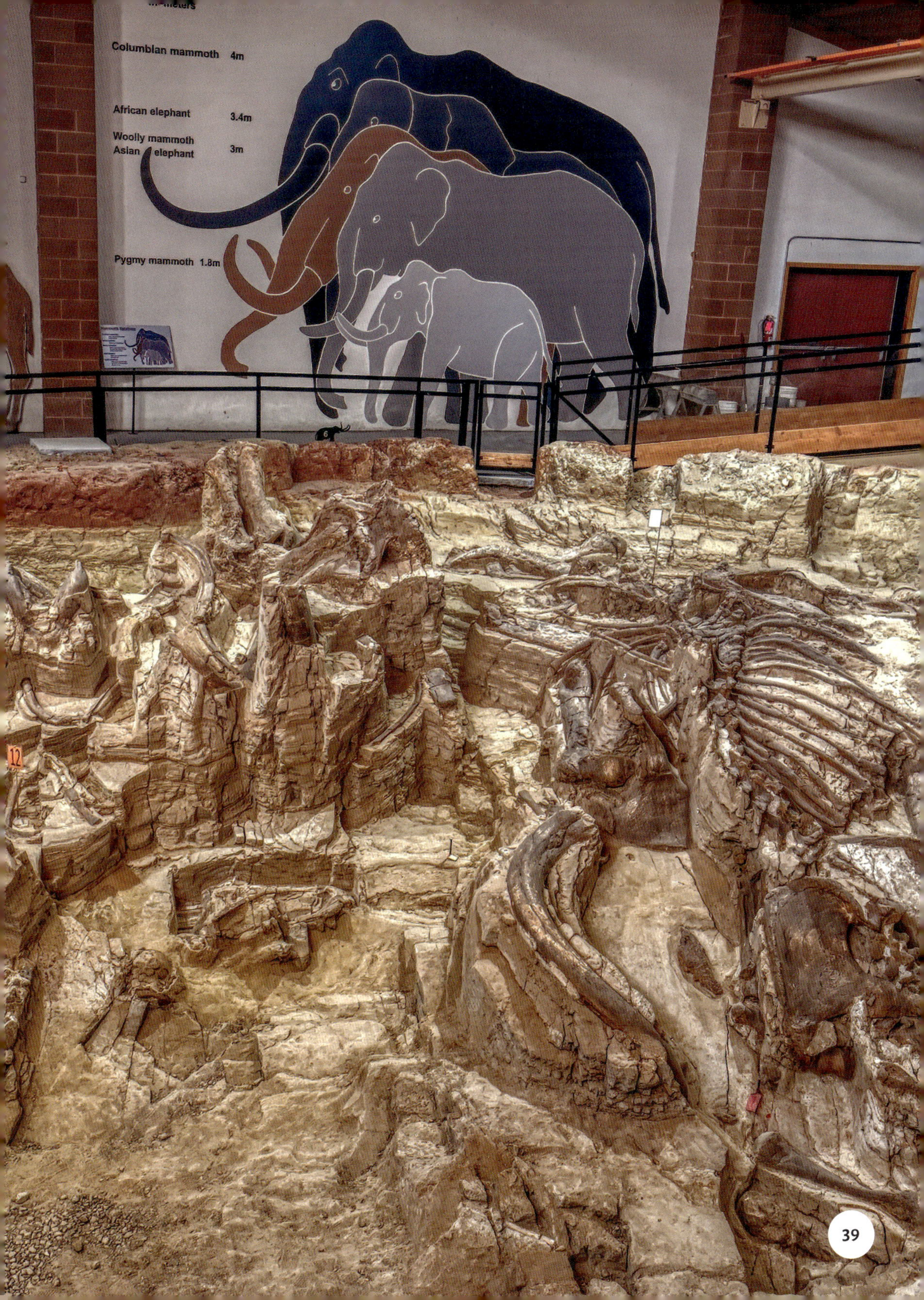
Columbian mammoth 4m
African elephant 3.4m
Woolly mammoth
Asian elephant 3m
Pygmy mammoth 1.8m

Visitors to South Dakota enjoy skiing in the Black Hills.

stunning views. South Dakota has six national parks and 56 state parks where visitors can enjoy the outdoors. They can boat, swim, hike, ski, and snowmobile. South Dakota offers many ways to explore.

STRAIGHT TO THE SOURCE

Jewel Cave was discovered in 1900 by brothers Albert and Frank Michaud, along with their friend Charles Bush. Two years later a promotional tourism book told the story of the cave's discovery:

> *It was discovered in 1900 by the Michaud brothers, who were prospecting in Hell's canyon, one of the rockiest, most precipitous canyons and one of the most beautiful, notwithstanding its infernal name, in the Hills. They were letting themselves carefully down a chimney in the rocks . . . when one of them noticed a hole a couple of inches in diameter and called his brother's attention to it, saying: "There is the entrance to a cave." The brother began pulling away the earth with his hand when the strong current of air blew a cloud of dust in his face. They knew so strong a current could come only from an immense cavern, and that they had indeed discovered a cave of great extent.*

Source: Jackie Gonzales and Emily Greenwald. "A Small Cave No More." *National Parks Service*, 2020, npshistory.com. Accessed 9 Aug. 2021.

CONSIDER YOUR AUDIENCE

Write a blog post conveying this same information for a new audience. How does your post differ from the original text and why?

IMPORTANT DATES

About 10,000 years ago
The first known people live in the area that is now South Dakota.

1832
Europeans establish Fort Pierre in the South Dakota region.

1874
Settlers flock to the Black Hills in search of gold.

1889
South Dakota becomes the thirty-ninth or fortieth US state on November 2.

1890
The Wounded Knee Massacre occurs.

1927
The carving of Mount Rushmore begins.

1920s
Drought begins to dry up the South Dakota landscape in the Dust Bowl.

1941
Mount Rushmore is completed.

1973
The Wounded Knee siege occurs.

2019
More than 14 million tourists visit South Dakota.

STOP AND THINK

Tell the Tale

Chapter Five mentions the discovery of South Dakota's Jewel Cave. Imagine you are exploring the landscape and you come across the entrance to a giant unexplored cave. Write 200 words about your discovery. How would you react? What would you do? Be sure to include plenty of detail in your narrative.

Dig Deeper

After reading this book, what questions do you still have about South Dakota's history? With an adult's help, find a few reliable sources that can help you answer your questions. Write a paragraph about what you learned.

You Are There

This book discusses Mount Rushmore. Imagine you are going to visit the famous mountain monument. Write a letter home telling your friends about your experience. What did you see and hear on the visit? Be sure to add plenty of detail to your notes.

Another View

This book talks about South Dakota wildlife. As you know, every source is different. Ask a librarian or another adult to help you find another source about South Dakota. Write a short essay comparing and contrasting the new source's point of view with that of this book's author. What is the point of view of each author? How are they similar and why? How are they different and why?

GLOSSARY

agriculture
the practice of farming crops and livestock

crop
a plant grown to be used as food

dam
a barrier built to hold back water and raise its level

fertile
rich in nutrients for growing plants

glacier
a large body of ice that moves across land

hydroelectric
electricity generated from flowing water

migration
to move to a different location, usually as the seasons change

prairie
a large, open area of grassland

reservation
an area of land set aside for American Indian people

reservoir
a large natural or artificial lake used as a source of water

treaty
an official agreement between governments

ONLINE RESOURCES

To learn more about South Dakota, visit our free resource websites below.

Core Library CONNECTION
FREE! COMMON CORE MULTIMEDIA RESOURCES

Visit **abdocorelibrary.com** or scan this QR code for free Common Core resources for teachers and students, including vetted activities, multimedia, and booklinks, for deeper subject comprehension.

Booklinks NONFICTION NETWORK
FREE! ONLINE NONFICTION RESOURCES

Visit **abdobooklinks.com** or scan this QR code for free additional online weblinks for further learning. These links are routinely monitored and updated to provide the most current information available.

LEARN MORE

Conley, Kate. *Engineering Mount Rushmore*. Abdo, 2018.

O'Brien, Cynthia. *Encyclopedia of American Indian History and Culture*. National Geographic, 2019.

INDEX

About the Author

Helen Evans Walsh is the author of several books for young adults and children.